Ludwig Philippson, Maurice Mayer

**The crucifixion and the Jews**

Ludwig Philippson, Maurice Mayer

**The crucifixion and the Jews**

ISBN/EAN: 9783337147297

Printed in Europe, USA, Canada, Australia, Japan

Cover: Foto ©Lupo / pixelio.de

More available books at **www.hansebooks.com**

# THE

# CRUCIFIXION AND THE JEWS.

BY

## DR. L. PHILIPPSON.

TRANSLATED FROM THE GERMAN,

BY

## MAURICE MAYER,

OF THE NEW YORK BAR.

PHILADELPHIA:
JONES & HAMILTON, PRINTERS, 510 MINOR STREET.
5626.

# PREFACE.

The following essay, on a subject which has so painfully affected the whole house of Israel, cannot be otherwise than interesting to the serious inquirer, who cares more for the truth of history than the triumphant rule of a party, and, strange as it may sound, Christianity is as yet but the latter, not catholic or universal as it generally vaunts to be. The death of its founder has been the theme on which millions of sermons have been delivered, and innumerable books written, and seldom is the subject touched but a denunciation, direct or implied, is uttered against our people, either for having knowingly rejected their redeemer or messiah, or with the crime of having murderously and treacherously put him to death. For either cause the Israelites are then condemned,—for the first to eternal perdition and unquenchable hell-fire, and for the second to the hatred and malice of their fellow-men. Now, it has happened strangely that under both causes we have been slaughtered without mercy, at times under the plea that our bodies must suffer for the purification of our souls, and again that we, the descendants of the early culprits, might make atonement for the guilt of our fathers.

Now, with the progress of a more enlightened policy on the part of all religionists in nearly all portions of the civilized world, it has become unusual to persecute for a simple difference of opinion on disputed points of theology; but thus far the world has not progressed to lay aside this difference as a matter which should not influence the feelings of one man towards the other. It is thus that writers and preachers, though they cannot well bring about a renewed indiscriminate massacre and plunder of Israelites, still succeed in keeping up a frightful amount of popular prejudice against those who are descended from the men who, more than eighteen centuries ago, are said to have urged Pontius Pilate to execute the founder of the popular belief. It was, no doubt, with the view of exhibiting the wrongfulness of this procedure that Dr. Ludwig Philippson, the celebrated editor of the *Allgemeine Zeitung des Juden-thums*, during the past year, wrote this treatise in detached portions for his paper, and as they naturally attracted attention, he issued them later in a pamphlet, for better preservation. The value of this work having likewise struck Dr. Maurice Mayer, of New York, he had the kindness to translate the same for the pages of the *Occident*, wherein the whole appeared during the space of six months. As Dr. Philippson had expressed a wish that his new contribution to Jewish literature should also become accessible to those who speak English, which wish was conveyed through Rabbi II. Hochheimer, of Baltimore, the subscriber resolved to gratify him in this reasonable desire, and now presents this tract to the kind consideration of the public, in the fond expectation that this small edition of five hundred copies may soon be exhausted, and a much larger new one be demanded. He would merely observe that it is not the intention to make any one unfaithful to Christianity, but merely to let this tract serve as a fender against the assaults of prejudice. The subject has not been thoroughly exhausted by Dr. Philippson; but enough has been shown that the Jews did *not* crucify the author of Christianity, at least in the sense which is usually attached to the expression, since crucifixion was not a Jewish but a Roman punishment. But granted even that the instigation came from the Jews, it was for the cause that an acknowledged and undisputed blasphemy required the punishment of death on the verdict of Jewish judges. No evidence exists that a messiah, supposed to be one, and so acknowledged by the Hebrew people, was molested or rejected by them; since the Gospels even do not assert that Jesus, in direct terms, ever claimed to be their expected redeemer, much less a god.

It should be noticed that the title has been somewhat modified from what the separate papers in the *Occident* bore, as it was somewhat awkward in an English dress, though it was more expressive than the one adopted for the present publication.

ISAAC LEESER.

*Elul* 5, *August* 16, 5626.

# THE CRUCIFIXION AND THE JEWS.

THE following essay, which at first appeared in the *Allgemeine Zeitung des Judenthums*, (*Universal Gazette of Judaism*,) and a separate publication of which has been generally desired,* *is no controversial work*, and does not pretend to belong to the department of Polemics. It seeks, in a simple and, so far as possible, objective manner, to arrive at a solution of the question upon which it treats. It is far from being offensive. It does not controvert the religious dogmas of others; for not even the dogma of redemption through the death of Jesus depends upon the issue of the inquiry whether or not the Jews were the authors of his death? On the contrary, our essay is intended to further peace between the professors of different religions, by removing an accusation—unjust as we deem it—which has spread animosity abroad, and caused discord and hostility. It has for its object to revise a legal proceeding, to re-examine the records still extant concerning it; it propounds again the question : Is the condemnation imposed upon a whole people, and the cruel consequence of which fifty generations have had to bear, justified or unfounded? That we are justified to institute such inquiry, that not alone the Jews but the whole Christian world are interested therein, is evident. Through many centuries the same cry has resounded which has subjected the Jews to so many persecutions, and instilled prejudice and hatred into Christian hearts.

But our age has arrived at the conviction, that an allegation must not be regarded as undoubted merely because it has been repeated through so many centuries, and so many errors have been proven as errors, although they had been no less under the protecting shield of old age, that it may not be inappropriate to

* We translate from the pamphlet.—TRANSLATOR.
1

enter upon our inquiry with an unprejudiced mind, and subject it to a new, more thorough investigation. Of course, we know beforehand that we shall not succeed in convincing all, who will favor the following pages with their perusal, of the correctness of our results. It is, indeed, a hard thing for man entirely to wean himself from a preconceived opinion which he has imbibed from his earliest infancy, which has been communicated and instilled into him by many men upon whom he can place especial reliance, pre-eminently so, indeed, when his opinion touches or even rests upon the realms of faith. But we shall be satisfied, if our most inveterate adversaries will but admit that we have been justified in discussing the question under consideration, and that we have remained within the bounds of strict impartiality and justice.

It had been our intention long ago to publish a full consideration of the subject before us, when we were induced to do so by a letter from a man who had been trained in general literature, from which we will extract the following passages:

"I was lately asked in what manner crucifixion was effected among the Jews, and how criminals were executed? Not being versed in the Talmud, and finding no information in the Bible, I was compelled to leave the question unanswered, and would, therefore, request you to communicate to me all that is most worthy of knowing upon the subject, and this, too, through the public press."

The question here is limited in its terms merely to ascertain, "How was the death penalty by crucifixion executed among the Jews?" We shall take it in a more extended acceptation, to wit: Whether and how far the Jews caused the crucifixion of Jesus? In treating upon the subject we shall proceed as follows: At first, we intend to reply to the question as our friend proposed it to us; then, we shall take a survey of the manner in which *our* question has been answered by others in our time, and, lastly, we shall present and authenticate our own views.

## I.

The question, In what manner the death penalty by crucifixion was executed among the Jews? must be simply answered thus: *It did not exist at all among the Jews.* Crucifixion was no Jewish death penalty, either according to Biblical or Talmudical law, and, considering the tenacity with which the Jews particularly adhered to their law, no Jewish tribunal could pronounce the punishment of crucifixion, nor could crucifixion ever be carried out by Jews. Crucifixion, on the other hand, was in use among the *Romans*, and even the Jewish law which commanded that a man suspended on a tree should be taken down before the beginning of the succeeding night, mitigated the Roman abuse, which allowed the sufferings of the crucified to continue for three, ay, even for seven days. If, then, a crucifixion took place in the Holy Land during the domination of the Romans, it. could not have been caused and executed by the Jews, but solely by the Romans, since, on the contrary, the Jewish law alleviated the fate of the unfortunates. We should refer our readers on this subject to *Jahn, Archæology* ii. 2, page 370.

According to the Mosaic law there existed three kinds of capital punishment, to wit : by the sword, (הרג,) by stoning, (סקילה,) and by burning to death, (שרפה.)* In what manner these capital punishments were executed in the practice of later times is described by Tradition in *Sanhedrin* vi., vii. Hanging is nowhere commanded as a capital punishment in the Pentateuch, but as it is ordained in *Deuteronomy* xxi. 22, 23, that "if a man have committed a sin worthy of death, and he be put to death and hanged to a tree, his body shall not remain all night upon the tree," it has been assumed that it was a custom to hang the corpse of an executed criminal. Tradition, farthermore, concluded, from verse 23, that such was the case only when a man suffered death by stoning. (*Sanhedrin* fol. 45, *b.*) Tradition also added a fourth death penalty, *strangulation* (חנק), for such crimes for which the Bible simply prescribes death penalty. (*Sanhedrin* vii. 3.)

*Thus, then, crucifixion as a capital punishment was entirely prohibited among the Jews.†*

## II.

However, we have gained little for our question by the proof

---

* The last-named took place only in two cases : when a man married a woman and her daughter at the same time, and when the daughter of a priest profaned her body.

† See our "Israelitish Religion," vol. iii., p. 177, and following. Leipzig: 1865.

that crucifixion was no legal capital punishment among the Jews, and that, therefore, it was never executed by them; for it is sufficiently known that, at the time under consideration, the Jews were under the rule of the Romans, and that criminal jurisdiction was entirely in the hands of the latter. Nevertheless, the Jews could, for all that, have directly caused the execution of Jesus, which was thereupon accomplished by the Romans in their own way. The former might not themselves have laid hand upon the person of Jesus, but have been, nevertheless, the real authors of his death. And it is even this thing that is charged upon them. Nor do we desire to lay any stress upon the fact that, since the Romans possessed the power, and had to confirm and execute or reverse the decision of the Jewish tribunal, a portion of the guilt must be charged upon them; for it could be replied, that if the Jews had been independent, they would themselves have executed the judgment, though not by means of crucifixion.

Our question, then, divides itself into two parts: 1. How far do we stand, with regard to the whole proceeding, upon a truly historical foundation, so that the whole case possesses the character of credibility? 2. If it be indeed historical, in what aspect will the motives and the proceedings in this trial, and with them the guiltiness or justification of the Jewish judges and leaders who had taken part therein, as well as of the people of that time, present themselves? We emphasize the phrase *of that time*, though it is in our time unnecessary to point out that, even if a heavy guilt should be proven upon the judges and leaders of the people of that time, their descendents, the subsequent generations of the Jews, have had no share in that guilt, and no unborn race can be made responsible for the actions of a past age. Upon this point we opine no thinking man entertains any doubt. Such being the rule concerning all departments of history, and touching the posterity of all nations, why should the Jews form an exception? The annals of all nations contain blood-drenched pages, present scenes of terror affecting distinguished individuals or whole classes; but after the authors of such atrocities have passed away from the scene of life, after their instruments have gone, and the motives which prompted their crimes have vanished, are then the following generations still made to sigh beneath the burden of condemnation? are they still despised for what was done in the past, long ago buried? But *this* consideration alone we must emphasize, that, if we desire to be just, we must not place ourselves upon a general humane, or rather, modern stand-point, to judge of the motives and proceedings in that trial as far as the actors are concerned; since it pre-eminently concerns us to ascertain whether the proceedings were legal, and the decision according to the laws then in force.

In examining our question, it was customary primarily to proceed from the second above-described premise, and the first was arrived at only at a later time. And this was natural; since it is well known that there is not a single historical report, not a single contemporaneous record in existence touching the whole proceeding, so that we are exclusively confined to the narratives of the Apostles.

In former times, however, no doubt was entertained as to the unconditional credibility of these narratives, and the first writers who undertook an examination of our subject were, therefore, compelled to attempt a demonstration of the motives and proceedings in that trial from the materials offered by the reports of the Apostles, without attacking in the least the reliability of their whole testimony.

It is from this point of view that also *Salvador*, in his "History of the Mosaic Institutions," book iv., chapter 3, treats the subject under consideration. He says: "My question, which can admit of no equivocation, is solely and exclusively this: 'Did the Jews, after having acknowledged him as a simple citizen, try him according to the ruling laws and forms of procedure, or not?' In my examination I take all the facts from the Gospels themselves, without investigating the question, whether the whole story had not been developed at a later period, with a view of giving form to a new doctrine, or to an old one to which a greater range was attributed." He observes farthermore: "Whether the law was good or bad, whether the forms of procedure were proper or improper, I do not now examine any farther." The essential momentum, then, which Salvador proposes to himself to deduce is this: *How* did the Jews of that time understand the words and speeches of Jesus? And the result to which he arrives is this, that they did most directly understand him to allege that he was *God*. Salvador says: " Jesus speaks of himself as of God. His disciples repeat this allegation, and the course of events proves, beyond all doubt and cavil, that they so understood him. This was a terrible blasphemy in the eyes of the Jewish people. The law commands to cleave to the One Eternal, never to believe in gods of flesh and bone, that resemble men or women, neither to listen to, nor to spare prophets, even if they gave a sign˚or a wonder, who should proclaim a new god,—a god whom they and their fathers had not known." (*Deut.* iv. 15, xiii.) Salvador, at the same time, refers to the Apostles themselves, (*John* vi. 39, 42, *Matthew* xiii. 55,) how the Jews murmured at the assertion of Jesus, that he had descended from heaven to accomplish all these things; how the people intended to stone him to death, and declared to do so, "for blasphemy, and because that thou, being a man, makest thyself God." (*John* x. 33.) Salvador adds: "Should it be asserted, however, in order to find a charge against the Jews, that Jesus did not directly represent himself as God, this question may be asked in reply: 'Why, then, do you *believe* he was a God? how was it possible that he was so understood, that his disciples so understood him?'" Does not the Church, even at this day, condemn every man who would take the words of Jesus in another sense? The Gospels, then, clearly show that the people could not but so understand Jesus, and did so understand him; that his words appeared to them as the greatest blasphemy, which the law punished with death. In a political respect, Salvador continues, the speeches of Jesus naturally created great dissensions among the people, and gave rise to the apprehension that the Romans would, on that account, oppress the country and its inhabitants, and that the whole nation might be destroyed. (*John* xi. 47, 50.) The Senate, therefore, assembled solely to deliberate,—and this was done publicly,—whether Jesus should be summoned before them. When this had been done, witnesses were examined, and these testified to a speech of Jesus, which John himself declared to be genuine. (*John* ii. 19.) The accused is then examined, as follows: (*Matthew* xxvi. 63, &c.) "And the high-priest answered, and said to him, 'I adjure thee, by the living God, that thou tell us whether thou be the Christ, the son

of God ?' Jesus saith unto him : ' Thou hast said ; nevertheless
I say unto you, Hereafter shall ye see the Son of man sitting at
the right hand of power, and coming in the clouds of heaven.'
Then the high-priest rent his clothes, saying: ' He hath spoken
blasphemy; what farther need have we of witnesses ? Behold!
now ye have heard his blasphemy.' " Thereupon they proceeded
to deliberate, and the Senate decided according to *Deuteronomy*
xiii. 16, *Leviticus* xxiv, 16. Pilate appeals to the people, but
they confirm the decision of the Senate. Salvador farthermore
examines all the details of the judical proceeding, and finds it
throughout in accordance with the law, whereas the indignities
offered to Jesus did not proceed from the Jews, but·from the Romans.

This exposition of Salvador created great sensation, and many
essays were published both in France and Germany, partly con-
firming, partly controverting his views. It was especially M.
Dupin l'aîné, who appeared against him with a refutation, intended to show that the whole trial was but the work of blindest
hatred, of violence and treachery. But his arguments were so
weak, his premises so slight, his quotations so faulty, and some-
times even,—in a true lawyer style,—so much garbled, that his
work created no effect.

The result of the investigation from the above-described stand-
point, as established in Germany, may be seen from two works.
On the Christian side, Winer, in his " *Biblisches Realwörterbuch*"
(Biblical Encyclopedia), transcribed Salvador's opinion, and then
continues : " Thus far it may appear that every thing is right.
Nor was the examination of the witnesses not a searching one,
(*Matthew* xxvi. 60,) and what the witnesses deposed, Jesus had
indeed spoken. (*John* ii. 19.) But that Jesus could not be the
Messiah, the members of the Sanhedrin judged from their views
concerning Christology, so that no blame can be attached to
them. A more accurate examination of the doctrines and acts
of Jesus, would, no doubt, have removed their error, that Jesus
was a blasphemer, and, perhaps, led them to correct their Messianic hopes. And here there is a point of view *for us*, from
which blame may be deservedly attached to the judges" Winer-
then concludes : " Thus, then, the condemnation itself deserves

less blame than this, that the High Court did not better inform itself, as it would have been worthy of its dignity, concerning the accused.

However much we must be satisfied that the learned Christian theologian reduces the ancient condemnation of the Jews to a mere "blame,"—and Winer does not, indeed, do it from predilection for the Jews,—this blame, nevertheless, appears unjustified; for, according to the above quoted clear passages, the Senate did not find Jesus guilty on account of his allegation that he was the Messiah, but on account of his professed doctrine of his divinity, which was in conflict with the whole Jewish idea of the unity and incorporeality of God.

On the part of the Jews it is *Saalschütz,* who, in his "Mosaic Law," (2d ed., Berlin, 1853,) vol. ii., p. 623, sought to fortify Salvador's view. He briefly repeats the arguments of his predecessor, and merely elaborates the second point, that referring to the political question. He observes: "The regal anointment of Jesus by a woman is approved by him. (*Matthew* xxvi. 7, 10.) His solemn entrance into Jerusalem is connected with this. Great multitudes came to meet him, and his disciples proclaimed him to be the son of David, the King, during all of which Jesus went into the Temple, overthrew the tables of the money changers, and drove out all those that there offered doves and other sacrificial animals for sale, (just as the wants of the pilgrims gave rise, in later times, to markets, "fairs," near the Christian churches.) (*Matthew* xxi. 1, 13, *Mark* xi. 1, &c., *Luke* xix. 30, &c., *John* xii. 12, xiii, 2, 13, &c.)

"This commotion created among the people by Jesus' disciples, and which he, convinced of his higher mission, approved in opposition to the warning words of some Pharisees, (*Luke* xix. 39, 40,) as also his mode of procedure in the Temple, prompted by the conviction of his own supreme power, caused great apprehension in the minds of the leaders of the people, informed thereof by witnesses, especially because they knew that the Romans were on the alert for new pretexts for their interference. And, indeed, the members of the highest tribunal give utterance to this apprehension, that Jesus might gain many adherents from the people, and that, in consequence, 'the Romans shall come

9

and take away both our place and nation.' (*John* xi. 47, 48.) Caiphas, the high-priest, then remarks: ' It is better for us that one man should die than that the whole people should perish.' (*Ibid.* xi. 49, 51.) It is certain that the Apostles expected the establishment, by Christ, of a worldly power and worldly dignities, and, even after his death, hoped for his speedy return to found a millennium on earth, all of which was confirmed by Jesus himself. (*Matthew* xvi. 27, 28, xix. 27, &c., xxiv. 29, 34, xxvi. 27, 29.) (*Compare, also, De Wette, Bibl. Dogm.*, p. 195.) Hence, it is natural that those who were farther removed from him than his disciples, supposed that he acted from political motives." So far Saalschütz. But, in order to make his views still more clear and proven, he ought to have examined also the conditions of that time, that many local revolts had taken place in different parts of Judea, and had been suppressed by the Romans with relentless rigor, so that we can easily understand the apprehensions of the Sanhedrin, in a political point of view.

These, then—referring for all details to the cited works themselves—are the results of the purely legal investigations, which demonstrate from the gospels themselves the motive and judicial proceeding, and justify them as being fully in accordance with the law.

### III.

Thus far even those could follow us who attribute full and literal credibility to the accounts of the gospels. They must be convinced, from our No. I., that the death penalty by crucifixion was against the Jewish law, and could not have been executed by the Jews. They must perceive, from our No. II., that the trial and condemnation were in accordance with the provisions of the Jewish law. The court could not have disregarded the law without being *itself* illumined by a higher revelation. That it received no such revelation cannot be used even by the most faithful Christian as a charge against it; for such an illumination was with God, and not in the power of the members composing the court. Nay, even from a Christian dogmatic stand-point, such a revelation could by no means have been vouchsafed to the Sanhedrin, otherwise the death of Jesus would not have taken

2

place, and the dogmatic mission of Jesus, according to the Christian doctrine, could not thus have been fulfilled. As soon, then, as it is proven that the judges did not act illegally, even the most faithful Christian cannot condemn them, because their dogmatic "blindness" was not and could not be removed by a higher revelation. Judges and people proceeded from their understanding of the speeches of Jesus, from the view taken of them by his disciples, by the whole Christian church, and they even, his speeches we mean, rendered him guilty according to law. The whole farther process of his trial and execution offered no circumstance that could shake or even weaken the conviction of the people and judges.

However, it is a known fact, that for a long time past the historical reliability of the gospel account has been doubted and subjected to critical investigations. These doubts and investigations have not proceeded from the Jews. They have developed themselves in and from the bosom of Christianity itself. They could not be avoided in the progressive development of the European world. But the Jews have no cause to disregard this criticism; for, considering that, from a religious point of view, they have no motive to accord unconditional belief to the gospel accounts, they are naturally attracted by such criticism. Hence, we have arrived at the first stage of our question : How far are we on really historical grounds, with regard to the death of Jesus ? This question is the more natural, because—1. No contemporaneous historian, nor one living near the time of Jesus, has left any records of his life and death, so that we are exclusively limited to the accounts of the Evangelists, who, at the same time, are a *party* in the case ; and because—2, these Evangelists often contradict each other in their accounts, exhibit variations which the most ingenious commentators have failed to reconcile, so that their *historical* genuineness becomes doubtful from the very beginning.

There are especially two passages in the writings of earlier non-Christian historians that make mention of Jesus.* The one occurs in Josephus' "Jewish Antiquities," xviii. 3, §3. But we hardly need observe that all impartial and even many partial critics

---

* The casual allusion to Christ in *Plinius epist.* x. 97, *Lamprid vit. Alex. Sever.* 29, 43, Lucian. de morte Peregr. 11, 13, is of no historical value.

have acknowledged that this passage was ~~not written~~ by Josephus, but interpolated by a later writer.* For, although even Eusebius quotes this passage, (*II. E.* i. 11, demonstr. ev. iii. 7,) it must be remembered that he lived from 267–340, C. E., and there was sufficient reason up to his time for interpolating such a passage into the work of Josephus, which was then extensively known, so that such a reliable witness could be referred to. But, as it always happens, whoever intends to prove too much testifies against himself. Both external and internal evidence prove that this passage was *not* composed by Josephus. As to external evidence, it is introduced in a manner that it destroys the whole context, being connected with neither the preceding nor the following passages. In the preceding paragraph mention is made of a sedition of the Jews at Jerusalem, which Pilate suppressed by cunning and violence. In the following the offence of some wicked persons at Rome is related, in consequence whereof many Jews were expelled from that city. The preceding narrative concludes with the words, "And thus was an end put to this sedition," and the following begins thus, "About the same time also another sad calamity befell the Jews." Now, any one reading the intervening passage, quoted in the note, will at once perceive that the thread of the historical narrative is thereby completely broken. "*Another* sad calamity" (§ 4) can refer only to the "sedition," (§ 2,) and thus completely excludes the contents of § 3. .The internal evidences are still stronger. It is impossible that Josephus should have said " He was the Christ," otherwise he must have professed himself to be a Christian, of which profession neither the passage under consideration nor any other presents the least trace. On the contrary, every expression of

* This passage reads as follows: " Now, there was about this time Jesus, a wise man, if it be lawful to call him a man ; for he was a doer of wonderful works, a teacher of such men as receive the truth with pleasure. He drew over to him both many of the Jews and many of the gentiles. He was the Christ. And when Pilate, at the suggestion of the principal men amongst us, had condemned him to the cross, those that loved him at the first did not forsake him ; for he appeared to them alive again on the third day, as the divine prophets had foretold these and thousand other wonderful things concerning him. And the tribe of Christians, so named from him, are not extinct at this day."

Josephus, in matters of religion and law, is in such direct conflict with that assumption, (Josephus consistently proves himself to be such a faithful votary of Jewish faith and Jewish law,) that it must be evident, even to the most prejudiced, that his sentiments cannot be reconciled with such an allegation.

For this reason some Christian critics would strike those words from the paragraph to save the rest. But the subsequent sentence, "He appeared to them alive again on the third day," can as little have proceeded from the pen of the believing Pharisee, which Josephus avows himself to be, as the doubt whether Jesus could be called a "man," or the application of the prophesies to Jesus, which latter sentiment, by the way, is in full keeping with the tendency of the Gospels.

The other passage occurs in Tacitus, (born 54, consul 97 a. C. E.) *Annales* xv. 44, § 4. In it mention is made of the great conflagration at Rome during the reign of Nero, and that this cruel, mad tyrant charged the Christians as its authors, and punished them accordingly.* The passage under consideration simply states that Christ had been executed through the procurator Pontius Pilate, under the reign of Tiberius. It is, as we shall have yet occasion to observe, of some importance for us, although its historical value might appear to be but insignificant, since Tacitus presents this statement, not in a historical narrative, but merely as a note, proceeding from the Christians themselves, with the view to explain their name.

This will suffice to show that all extraneous historical evidence for the life of Jesus are wanting. All later writers draw exclusively from Christian sources, which again are based upon the Gospels alone. Nor have the Talmudical notices concerning Jesus any historical value, because they are not founded upon direct

---

* *Ergo abolendo rumori Nero subdidit reos, et quæsitissimis pœnis affecit, quos per flagitia invisos, vulgus Christianos appellabat. Auctor nominis ejus Christus, qui imperio imperitante, per procuratorem Pontium Pilatum supplicio affectus erat.*"

"Therefore, in order to remove the rumor, Nero accused and punished with the most exquisite penalties those who, hated on account of their vices, were commonly called Christians. The author of this name was Christus, who was · executed through the procurator Pontius Pilatus, during the reign of Tiberius."

13

traditions, but have their origin in later times and follow Christian traditions. Why, they do not even agree with regard to the time in which Christ lived. Some represent him to have lived a century before his time; others at the time of the destruction of the Temple. (*Sanhedrin*, 107 *b*; *Midr. Echa*, 59; *Jer. Berach*, 5 *a*. Compare *Jost, History of Judaism*, Vol. I., page 404.)

Amongst those who have subjected the historical credibility of the four Gospels to a careful and sharp criticism, *David Frederick Strauss* occupies the foremost position, owing both to his well known work, published in 1836, entitled "The Life of Jesus," and to the new edition of 1864, intended "for the German people." He states the result of his investigations, page 70, as follows: "Thus the review of the evidence with regard to the three first Gospels gives this result, That, soon after the beginning of the second century, certain traces are found of their existence, not, indeed, in their present form, but still of the presence of a considerable portion of their contents, and with every indication that the source of these contents is derived from the country which was the theatre of the events in question. On the other hand, the issue of the examination with regard to the fourth Gospel (John) is far less favorable, and goes to prove that it was not known until after the middle of the century, (the second,) and bears every indication of having arisen upon a foreign soil, and under the influence of a philosophy of the time unknown to the original circle in which Jesus lived. In the first case, it is true that the period between the occurrence of the events and the recording of them in their present form, amounts to several generations, and the possibility is not excluded that what is legendary and unhistorical may have crept in; but, in the latter, there is every probability of an admixture of philosophical combination and designed fiction."

Thus, then, according to Strauss, the four Gospels contain a certain historical foundation, which, however, was altered, reversed, and amplified by myths, prompted by the design both to represent prophetic, especially Messianic announcements, as having been literally fulfilled in the life of Jesus, and to add dogmas which had been adopted in later times in the Christian Church. In his opinion, then, all that should be done is this: To discover the historical element, which must be done, on one hand, by discarding all that is miraculous and supernatural, and, on the other, to separate from the contradictions and variations of the four Gospels all that concerning which they agree. Therefore, Strauss at first presents the "HISTORICAL OUTLINE OF THE LIFE OF JESUS," and then "THE MYTHICAL HISTORY OF JESUS ACCORDING TO ITS ORIGIN AND DEVELOPMENT."

Following these principles, he takes, as far as our subject is concerned, the following, as founded in history, (p. 284,) "In the succeeding narrative of the trial and condemnation of Jesus, (*Matt.* xxv. 57, xxvii. 31 ; *Mark* xiv. 53, xv. 20 ; *Luke* xxii. 54, xxiii. 25; *John* xviii. 12, xix. 16,) all the Evangelists have in common the following particulars : That Jesus was first tried by the Jewish authorities, found guilty, and then taken before the Roman procurator, who was to have confirmed and executed the sentence of death, but who, not being able immediately to convince himself of the guilt of the accused, made repeated attempts to save him, but yielded at last to the violent importunities of the Jews, and then gave the order for his crucifixion. The guilt of Jesus before the Jewish tribunal appears in the two first Gospels in the form of evidence, stated to be false, to the effect that he had said that he would destroy the Temple of God, and in three days build it up again, *i. e.*, as was explained above, he was accused of an attack upon the existing system of the Jewish religion. Now, this certainly, in the sense of any violent means that he might be supposed to have had in view, was a false accusation, but, as to the latter object, not altogether without foundation. Then he is asked whether he asserts himself to be the Messiah. He answers in the affirmative, appealing to *Psalms* cx. and *Daniel* vii. This is considered as blasphemy, and a crime worthy of death. In the presence of the Roman governor, the Jewish authorities availed themselves, according to the unanimous account of the Evangelists, of the political side, that, as the professed Messiah, he claimed to be the king of the Jews, in order to represent the accused in the character of an agitator of the people against the Roman power. In this, though not without difficulty, as Pilate could not discover in Jesus any signs of a man politically dangerous, they at last succeeded. In all this there is nothing historically improbable, though we cannot overlook the fact that the resistance of Pilate is worked out with especial industry by the Evangelists, in order to bring out into strong relief the innocence of Jesus on the one hand, and the obstinate wickedness of the Jews on the other. We shall return, therefore, to this subject in a subsequent examination, as well as to all the more accurate details of these scenes in the gospels."

Even here we must emphasize the fact that Strauss has no stronger designation for this historical extract than this, that it contains "nothing historically *improbable;*" but "*not improbable*" is a very weak argument in a historical narrative. Nevertheless, even here he must confess that a strong *party spirit* and *intentional exaggeration against* the Jews are evident, so that a certain dose of the improbable is added to the probable. And this he discovers himself in his *second* book. Here he finds the motive for the whole narrative : "That the condemnation of Jesus through the authorities of his own people, whose Messianic Redeemer he intended to become," that his delivery to the Roman procurator and his crucifixion must be destructive to the hope and belief of "even his followers belonging to that people," and that, therefore, they were compelled to change his trial and death, not to mention his resurrection, into an honor and prop of their faith. Therefore, it is asserted that the condemnation was pronounced upon false testimony, whereas John confirms this testimony, but that the witnesses had misunderstood him, that Jesus had not meant the Temple, but his own body. Therefore, it is repeated, that Jesus made no reply to the question of the high-priest nor to that of Pilate. Therefore, lastly, he solemnly declared, upon the question whether he was the Messiah, that he was the Messiah, so that, according to Christian views, the condemnation by the Sanhedrin uttered its own condemnation. The indignities and cruelties that followed were but to present the literal fulfillment of Isaiah l. 6. Now, as it became more and more evident, in the course of the spread of Christianity, that the Jews could not be won for it, that the Græco-Roman world was the proper field for its propagation, it was sought to represent the execution through the Roman procurator in a way as to clear him as much as possible from guilt, *and to heap all of it upon the Jews.* According to

Strauss this is entirely *unhistorical*, since Pilate either was fully convinced of the guilt of Jesus, or deemed it advantageous to comply this time with the desire of the Jews. In the latter case, considering that he publicly declared his conviction of the innocence of the accused, he publicly avowed himself a coward and weakling, and yet did not deserve the thanks of the Jews, because he thus placed them in a very bad light. Strauss then examines the whole history of the trial before Pilate, and shows the contradictions and intentional misrepresentations in every part of it. It is impossible for him to suppose that Pilate again and again attempts to save Jesus, and then testifies his innocence by the improvised ceremony of washing his hands, and still more improbable it appears that the assembled people should distinctly take upon themselves and their children the guilt of Jesus' death. The latter circumstance, it is evident to him, was clearly invented with the view to represent the terrible end of the Jewish commonwealth as the punishment visited upon the children for the crime of the shedding of Jesus' innocent blood by their fathers. But it is certain that Pilate could not thus publicly expose his own weakness and cowardice. The first Evangelist, indeed, felt this, and introduced, therefore, the warning dream of Pilate's wife. Luke introduces instead the history of the presentation of Jesus before Herod, to have Jesus declared innocent by two Judges, a Christian and a Jew.

As to details, we must refer our readers to the work of the acute critic itself. One thing only excites our astonishment,— that he did not feel himself impelled to adduce the historical records concerning the character and proceedings of Pilate, to derive from them a well founded conclusion that the narratives of the Evangelists are in direct conflict with his otherwise known character. We will here merely state the fact that, according to Strauss, the whole narrative of the trial before Pilate is unhistorical and an invention based on party motives, a result to which we must the more adhere, because it appears to us, from a comparison of the two parts of his work, that he had *unwillingly* arrived at the result, to clear the Jews from all guilt.

The author who, after Strauss, has gained the greatest renown in literature of this kind is the Frenchman *Ernest Rénan* (*Vie de Jésus, cinquième edition,* Paris: 1863); but for our subject he is of no value. Rénan is no critic, but merely rationalist. He has attempted to divest the life of the author of Christianity both of all that is miraculous and supernatural, and all irrational dogmas; all that for him then remains in the Gospels he regards as history. On that account he subjects the Gospels to no critical examination whatever. From the tales, speeches, and sentences thus remaining, as far as they can be divested of all that is mystical, he construes a life of Jesus. Contradictions and improbabilities do not embarrass him. As to the former, he adopts them unconsciously; as to the latter, he introduces them with the phrase, "Is it said," or, "According to a tradition;" or he passes both in silence. With the aid of lively colors, or psychological *raisonnements,* he, a master of his language, produces a very readable biography. It was natural, therefore, that his work found many readers, especially in France, and was met with violent refutation on the part of the clergy; but it could gain no great importance in the domain of science and historical criticism. For, after all, much of that work rests upon arbitrary assumption—very little upon critical principles and an examination corresponding with them. He assumes that there existed original documents written by Matthew and Mark, but which are no longer extant; that we have a simple compilation, in which the original documents are mixed up together without discrimination, and without regard to the personal intentions of their authors, and by this compilation he means the present Gospels according to Matthew and Mark; and lastly, that there is an intentional, well considered compilation, in which the effort to reconcile all different versions is manifest, to wit: the Gospel according to Luke. The Gospel according to John, our author regards as a later composition, made for dogmatical reasons, which are in complete conflict, both in form and spirit, with the other three Gospels (page 42). Whoever, therefore, intends to deduce a biography from such documents, without taking the trouble, at every step, to discriminate between what is historically certain and what is his-

3

torically improbable, must run into a subjective arbitrariness.
Thus Rénan presents to us a long narrative of the trial and condemnation (pp. 391–413), into which he has introduced all that
the four Evangelists have chronicled, without taking the least
notice of the contradictions, improbabilities, &c., which he ne-
cessarily meets, and wherever they appear too glaring he innocently seeks to explain them by psychological observations. Let
us adduce but one example. Pilate retires with Jesus into the
palace; no witness is present at the conversation between them,
yet it is related to us by John. For Strauss the contents of this
narrative have no historical value. Rénan thinks otherwise; for
"the purport of this conversation, in its details, appears to have
been well divined by John." Hence we cannot be astonished to
see it reproduced entire by Rénan in his narrative of the trial.
Rénan likewise often contradicts himself most glaringly, even
now and then on the same page of his book. On page 307 he
says: "From the stand-point of orthodox Judaism Jesus was
truly a blasphemer, a destroyer of the established worship, and
these crimes were, according to law, punished with death." Yet
on the same page we read, a little before, as follows: "The sentence was drawn up; pretexts only were sought. Jesus knew
it, and did not undertake a useless defence." Here, then, we
meet with a double contradiction; for if Rénan acknowledges
that the sentence was well founded and justified, both according
to the facts elicited and the law, he cannot regard it as having
been fixed beforehand, and afterwards so pronounced, and not
otherwise, in conflict with a thorough defence; and the silence of
Jesus was his confession, and, if he knew his innocence, was unjust, because he did not, by his action, prevent the Court from
perpetrating an unjust act. Thus, then, we have characterized
the opinion of Rénan. He narrates every thing found in the
Gospels, charges the whole guilt upon the Jews, and seeks, by
means of a large expenditure of phrases and hypotheses, to clear
Pilate; yet he finds that the sentence of the Jewish Court was
justified according to law, only he flings his accusation at the
law, and recognizes a just retaliation in the destinies of the Jewish nation. Meeting with such a confusion of ideas and such a
misconception of all history, we may dispense with all farther

examination. We said so much lest we should be charged with
an omission.

After Strauss it was especially the Tübingen school that presented itself in the domain of Gospel criticism, and started from
the idea that the struggle in the first time of Christianity between the Judaizing Christians and the heathen Christians may
be observed already in the Gospels, and gave rise to interpolations. The former, thus it is alleged by that school, intended to
remain within the pale of Judaism, would preserve the law, and .
have nothing to do with the heathens. The latter, on the other
hand, regarded the heathen world as the special sphere of Christianity, and desired to see the law abolished. The leader of the
latter was Paul. Many contradictions in the narratives of the
Evangelists may be explained by the various interpolations and
changes introduced by both parties. To arrive at a clear con-
ception of these was the intention of the Tübingen school.

On this ground the latest Jewish historian, *Dr. II. Grätz*, follows the critics. In a special chapter, entitled " *The Origin of
Christianity,*" in the second edition of the third volume of his
"*History of the Jews,*" he treats of this subject in an original
and ingenious manner, keeping, at the same time, within the
limits of moderate and considerate criticism. He has come to
the conclusion that the author of the Christian religion derived
his doctrines from the Essenes, and had been an adherent of that
sect. Let us now see how Grätz handles our subject.' Even
the narrative of Jesus' entry into Jerusalem he regards as legend-.
ary. " It is related that the people accompanied him in triumph
and with hosannahs to Jerusalem. But the same people are said
to have demanded his death a few days later. Both these accounts are fictions ; the former with the view to represent his re-
cognition by the people as the Messiah, and the latter to charge
the blood-guiltiness of his execution upon the whole people of
Israel. The relations which Jesus occupied in Jerusalem with
the people, the Sanhedrin, and the different sects, is enveloped
in profound darkness, and the reasons for which he was hated
and persecuted by the Jews are nowhere made clear. His pecu-
liar mode of proceeding was indeed in conflict with the expecta-
tions then current among the people concerning the hoped for

Messiah. He may have offended the Shammaites* by his healing the sick on Sabbath ; his speeches against the wealthy offended the rich and men of rank ; and his admonitions to be peaceful towards the Romans enraged the zealots. " But all these offences afforded as yet no ground for an accusation against him; hence he could not be proceeded against. Free expression of opinion had become such a deep-rooted custom, through the frequent debates of the Academies of Shammai and Hillel, that no one could be persecuted on account of his dissenting religious opinion, as long as he did not violate generally acknowledged religious laws, or expressed himself against the Jewish idea of the divinity." Hence the latter point alone was left. Grätz thinks it contradictory that the betrayal of Judas, by means of a kiss, was necessary to point out the man who is said to have entered Jerusalem in triumph, and publicly preached in the Temple. " The trial consisted in this, that the Court desired to establish the fact, whether Jesus did proclaim himself the Son of God, as the witnesses had testified. It seems entirely incredible that he should have been tried for this, that he had before proclaimed, he could destroy the Temple and build it up again within three days. Such an expression, even if he had indeed used it, could not have been made a cause of accusation. On the contrary, the charge was that of *blasphemy* (*Gidduf*, βλασφημια), whether Jesus meant to be acknowledged as the Son of God." Upon the question repeatedly put to him Jesus gave the well known answer. "Pilate, before whom Jesus was brought, inquired of him after the political meaning of his course, whether he, as the Messiah, represented himself as the king of the Jews, and when Jesus gave the equivocal reply, 'Thou sayest it,' the procurator simply confirmed the verdict. This alone was what he had to do. That Pilate had found Jesus innocent, and desired to save him, but that the Jews had insisted upon his death, is a legendary embellishment. If Jesus was scorned at, and compelled to wear a crown of thorns as a mocking of his Messianic royalty, this atrocity was not caused by the Jews, but by the

* The adherents of the Academy of Shammai, which represented *strict* observance of the law (with insignificant exceptions); whereas the Academy of Hillel taught a *milder* practice, which indeed gained the ascendency.

Roman soldiers, who were glad to deride the Jewish nation through him. The Jewish judges entertained so little factious hatred against his person, that the cup with wine and incense was offered to him, as to every other condemned person, with the view to benumb his senses, and thus mitigate the agonies of death. According to the then valid criminal law, a man found guilty of blasphemy was first to be stoned to death, and then nailed to the cross. Undoubtedly, Jesus was crucified in the same manner, but then he was dead already before his crucifixion." Grätz adds: " Such was the end of the man who labored for the moral improvement of his people, and became the victim of a misunderstanding. His death became the cause, though innocently, of numberless sufferings and manifold manners of death among the sons of his people. He is the only man, born of woman, of whom we may say without exaggeration, 'He has accomplished more by his death than by his life.' "

A step farther in criticism has been taken very recently by *Dr. S. Hirsch*, Grand Rabbi of Luxemburg, with whose exposition we will close our historical review. In the April and May numbers of the "*Archives Israélites,*" the said author publishes an opinion concerning the question, Whether the Jews are commanded to have separate burial places? On mentioning the crucifix as a customary symbol on Christian graves, Dr. H. makes a digression, and treats on the subject under consideration. At first he calls the attention of the reader, as a point of especial moment, to the fact that, although the sects which, at the time of Jesus, divided Judaism, are often mentioned in the Gospels, the Evangelists, at the same time, show "that they never lived among those sects, that they knew them only from hearsay, and that they had derived all their knowledge concerning them from Josephus, whom they did not, however, understand at all." Dr. H. then proves, by ample argument, that Jesus coincided with the Pharisees, and must have found them to be his friends, touching his chief doctrine, the belief in the "Heavenly Kingdom," (מלכות שמים,) and its near advent, together with the specific dogmas connected therewith, especially that of resurrection,—whereas the Sadducees, who most peremptorily repudiated all these articles of faith, must have been the natural enemies of Jesus. But even the very converse is found in the Gospels, and the very fact that the Sadducees are mentioned, proves that the Evangelists had no knowledge whatever of them. We will pass over this point to quote what Dr. II. says of the death of Jesus: "The form of criminal procedure, as it was practised at the time when the Jews could yet judge of life and death, has been preserved to this day in the *Mishnah*. This form must the more be regarded as having been derived from tradition, as it was a rule among the Rabbis to establish no doctrines which had no longer any practical object in view, but could be observed only at the time of the Messiah (הלכתא למשיחא). Now, what does the *Misnah* tell us concerning that form of procedure? 'Whenever a man was tried for his life, a verdict of not guilty could be pronounced on the first day; but if he was to be condemned, the decision had to be postponed to the day after. For this reason, such a case could not be tried on the eve of Sabbath or a Festival. A criminal case could never be decided at night.'" (*Sanhedrin* 32.)

It is true, we find in a *Boraitha*, (*Tosiphtha Sanhedrin* 10,) that this form of procedure was not strictly observed when an enticer to idolatry (*Deuteronomy* xiii. 7–12) was tried, that the verdict could be pronounced on the first day or at night, provided, however, the trial had begun during the day. Now, Jesus could not have been regarded as an enticer to idolatry, and then this exception, touching such an offender, looks more than suspicious; indeed, it appears to me that it was borrowed from the very Gospels. As the Rabbis had heard from the Christians that the author of their religion had been crucified on the day preceding the Feast of Passover, (according to John,) or on the first day of that Festival, (according to the other three Evangelists,) and knowing that the Christian religion alleged to be a new religion, which abolished that of the Jews, they concluded that criminal procedure afforded less protection to those who intended to introduce a new religion. Why should the forms of jurisdiction, which had been established more in the interest of the falsely accused than the guilty, have been less observed the heavier the charges were? "Hence, Jesus could not, according to the laws of the Jews, have been tried either at night, as Matthew and Mark mean to make us believe, or on the day preceding the Passover, or on the Festival itself." According to the Evangelists, Jesus was condemned because he declared himself to be " Christ, the Son of God." " Indeed, in the eyes of the Evangelists, in the the eyes of the Christians of the second century, for whom Christ had become the ' God-man,' for whom the name ' Son of God ' designated the μονογενης, who knew that it was this very designation that appeared repulsive to the Jews,—in the eyes of the Christians his declaration to be the Son of God must appear as the greatest crime that could be brought to the cognizance of a Jewish tribunal. But it was by no means a crime in the eyes of Jesus' contemporaries. (*Exodus* iv. 26, *Deuteronomy* xiv. 1, 2 *Samuel* vii. 14.) Any pious man could claim this title.* What part did Pilate act, according to the Evangelists? With the view clearly to prove the malice of the Jews, that it was the Jews, and the Jews exclusively, who caused the death of Jesus, they do not hesitate to represent Pilate as the greatest coward that ever existed. He wished to save Jesus because he deemed him innocent. He made every attempt to save him ; but he yielded to the raving clamor of an excited populace, and delivered to them the Son of God, that he should be crucified." " But Philo of Alexandria, a contemporary of Jesus, presents to us quite a different character of the Roman procurator. ' Pilate,' he says, ' was very merciless, as well as very obstinate, by nature, who would do nothing to please the Jews.' (*Legatio ad Cajum, m. u.*, p. 590.) And Josephus shows that this governor well understood how to disperse an excited populace." (*Bell. Jud.* 11–18.)

" Thus, then, history knows little about the condemnation and execution of Jesus ; but one fact is settled, that he was crucified under Pontius Pilate; but of the events which are said to have caused and accompanied this catastrophe we know absolutely nothing. The Jews, that is to say the Jewish religion, men who were vested with the right and mission to pronounce sentence in the name of this religion, and to act accordingly, did by no means cause the condemnation of Jesus."

---

* Dr. Hirsch here far transgresses all bounds. According to Matthew, Mark, and Luke, Jesus did not stop with his allegation that he was the "Son of God," but added : "Hereafter shall ye see the son of man sitting on the right hand of power, and coming in the clouds of heaven." This is more than the mere title " Son of God," which any pious man could claim.

Thus far Dr. Hirsch. Let us now once more present our own examination of the whole proceeding.

## IV.

This much is settled : There are no historical records concerning the trial of Jesus. We have no other accounts than those of the Evangelists.

But the Gospels are by no means *historical*, but exclusively *religious* books, which were composed, transmitted, and shaped for dogmatical purposes. The authors of the Gospels were no contemporaries of Jesus, but lived more than a century later, and can claim no *historical* credibility, both on account of the many contradictions found between them, and because they introduced many elements of the wonderful.

As an historical fact, that only is established which Tacitus (*Annal.* xv. 44, §4) relates : "*Auctor nominis ejus* (*Christianorum*) *Christus, qui imperio imperitante, per procuratorum Pontium Pilatum supplicio affectus erat.*" "The author of the name of the Christians is Christus, who suffered death, under the reign of Tiberius, through the procurator Pontius Pilate."·

Now, on examining the accounts of the Evangelists, we arrive at this result : *That it was the Romans alone who, for political reasons, executed Jesus, because he presented himself as the Messiah among the Jews.* If we remove from the Gospels the account of the trial of Jesus before the Sanhedrin, and of the influence of the Jewish people upon his execution, all connection and explanation of the events is restored, and all contradictions are removed.

For this we have to furnish the proofs.

Passing over at once to the execution of Jesus, we are told by the Evangelists that, after his condemnation by Pilate, the Roman soldiers put on him a scarlet or purple robe, placed a crown of thorns on his head, and a reed in his right hand, bowed the knee before him, and mocked him, saying, "Hail, king of the Jews!" But when they had crucified him they " set up over his head his accusation, written, "*This is Jesus, the king of the Jews.*" (*Matthew* xxvii. 27–37, *Mark* xv. 16–20, *Luke* xxiii. 38, *John* xix. 2.) According to John (xix. 19) Pilate himself "wrote a title and put it on the cross, and the writing was, *Jesus of Nazareth, the king of the Jews.*" The Jews demurred to this inscription, but "that he had said, I am the king of the Jews," whereupon Pilate answered, "What I have written I have written." What conclusion can we derive from all this? Undoubtedly no other than that the Romans, with Pilate at their head, executed Jesus as a political offender against the Roman rule. They crucified him as "king of the Jews;" they mocked him as such by a purple robe, by a crown and a sceptre; they thus gave vent to their hatred, not alone against Jesus, but also against the Jewish people. Nay, the inscription composed by Pilate himself, and the obstinacy with which he insisted upon it, clearly show that Pilate thereby intended to represent the Jews as accomplices in the political crime, as he regarded it; whereas they desired every allusion to their complicity removed. (Pilate attempted the same thing before, and the Jews demurred to it. *John* xix. 14, 15.)

But not alone the execution of Jesus, his condemnation also by Pilate appears in the same light. Matthew (xxvii. 11) relates, "And Jesus stood before the governor, and the governor asked him, saying, 'Art thou the king of the Jews?' And Jesus said unto him, 'Thou sayest.'" The same is related by Mark (xv. 2) and Luke (xxiii. 3). According to John (xviii. 37) Pilate said to him, "Art thou a king then?" Jesus answered, "Thou sayest that I am a king." But was there sufficient reason to induce Pilate to regard Jesus as a king? And was he the man capable of ordering an execution for that reason? Whatever is related to us of the previous life of Jesus shows that he traveled about in Gallilee, teaching *without the least interruption, or serious interruption, on the part of the Jews*, that he did and said all he pleased, without being actually persecuted by them; that he, on the contrary, found many adherents among the people, and that those who were hostile to him only sought to render him suspicious before the people by putting captious questions to him. He goes to Judea. He approaches Jerusalem completely undisturbed. But now he enters the city in solemn procession, and this, too, in literal.fulfilment of an ancient prophecy, "Sitting upon an ass, and a colt, a foal of an ass." Great multitudes come to meet

4

him, spread their garments in the way, cut down branches from the trees, and strew them in the way, and the multitudes that go before and after him greet him with "Hosanna." The whole city is thrown into commotion and pay him homage. He goes into the Temple and drives all out who bought and sold objects of sacrifices, and overthrows the tables of the money-changers and seats of venders of doves. He harangues the multitude, chastises the Scribes and Pharisees, and seeks to awaken the belief in the people that he is the promised Messiah. (*Matthew* xxi., &c., *Mark* xi., &c., *Luke* xix. 20, &c.) The people believe him, "For," says Luke, (xix. 48,) "all the people were very attentive to hear him," and, although "the chief priests and the scribes and the chiefs of the people sought to destroy him, yet they feared the people;" they did not, therefore, venture to touch him. (*Luke* xix. 47, 48, xx. 19.) Considering the manner of his conduct in general, and his entrance into Jerusalem, the commotion of the people, which daily increased upon the speeches of Jesus, it was but a natural consequence that the Roman procurator, whose attention had, perhaps, been called to the affair, interfered, secured the person of Jesus, and condemned him upon his own confession. For this purpose a trial before the Sanhedrin, and the co-operation of the people were by no means required to bring about such an issue. Whatever opinion may be entertained of the *details* of the entrance of Jesus, all that we have pointed out shows that the commotion of the people in Gallilee and at Jerusalem had reached such a height, and the situation of affairs and Pilate's character were such, that the interference of the latter became a natural consequence.

We need not relate to those acquainted with history all the events that preceded the administration of Pilate as governor of Judea. The Jews endured with reluctance the yoke imposed upon them by the Romans. They were extremely irritated and sensitive, and ready for revolt and resistance. Pilate himself had, from the very beginning, refused to spare the feelings of the Jews, nurtured their indignation, and was, at any moment, ready to use the sword against them and cut them down. Speaking of an event not at all connected with our subject, Philo gives us a description of his character. "Pilate," he tells us, "was by nature inflexible and cruel, as well as relentless." (ην γαρ την φυσιν αχαμπης και μετα του αυθαδους αμειλικτος. *Legat. ad Caj. ed. Hoesch.*, page 1034.) He relates that Pilate, as governor of Judea, "not more with the object of doing honor to Tiberius than that of vexing the multitude, dedicated some gilt shields in the palace of Herod, in the holy city, which had no form nor any other forbidden thing represented on them, except some necessary inscription, which mentioned these two facts, the name of the person who had placed them there, and the person in whose honor they were so placed there." When this thing became known, he was entreated on all sides "to alter and rectify this innovation, and not to make any alteration in their national customs;" but he refused their petition harshly, and would not comply with their entreaties. Only once he yielded to the Jews, not from fear, but because the cause was not in proportion with the consequences to be expected. The case was this: He had brought his army to Jerusalem for winter quarters, and the standards, with the picture of the emperor upon them, carried to the city and set up there. As this was a violation of the Jewish law, no Roman governor had attempted the same thing before. The people went to Cæsarea in large multitudes, and entreated him for several days to remove the standards to some other place. He would not yield, ordered the soldiers secretly to arm themselves, and to surround the Jews, and then threatened to put them immediately to death if they would not quietly return to their houses. But the Jews threw themselves upon the ground, uncovered their necks, and declared that they would rather die than allow any thing contrary to their laws. Pilate was not willing to carry things to extremes, and ordered the standards to be removed to Cæsarea. Some time afterwards Pilate seized the Temple treasure, under the pretext to use it for the construction of an aqueduct. The people assembled and raised a loud clamor. Pilate sent a large number of soldiers, dressed in Jewish garments, with clubs concealed beneath, and these ferociously fell upon the clamoring populace, and slew a large number. "This atrocity," says Josephus, "brought the Jews to silence." (*Antiq.* xviii. 3, § 2, *Bell. Jud.* ii. 9, §§ 2–4.) Among the Samaritans a great commotion was stirred up by an imposter, who induced them to dig after some sacred vessels, which, as he stated, had been buried by Moses on Mount Gerizzim. Pilate anticipated them, stationed troops, horse and foot, on the road to the mountain. These cut down a portion, dispersed others, and made many captives, of whom Pilate had the most distinguished put to death. This massacre afforded the cause for his dismissal. The Samaritans proved to Vitellius, the governor of Syria, that they had no intention to rebel against the Romans, and he at once ordered Pilate to repair to Rome to defend himself against the charges made against him by the Jews. (*Antiq.* xviii. 4, § 1.) Let the reader remember also the conduct of Pilate, mentioned above, as described by John on the occasion of the inscription above the cross, and he will have a full picture of his relentlessness and hatred against the Jews.

For a man of such a character, and who thus clearly manifested his intentions and purposes, suspicion and a popular commotion already commenced were a sufficient pretext for ordering the execution of a man accused of seeking to usurp the rule over the people; and, indeed, the Roman governors were very watchful of every attempt to claim the Messiahship raised among the Jews. Wherever and whenever such an attempt was made they suppressed it with relentless rigor. Thus, a certain *Theudas* represented himself, in the year 46, as the Messiah, and won four hundred adherents. They went to the banks of the Jordan, which Theudas had promised to divide in the midst. But the Roman governor, Fadus, ordered a troop of cavalry to surprise them, and cut them down, and to behead Theudas. (*Josephus Antiq.* xx. 5, § 1.) During the administration of Felix, an Egyptian Jew called upon the people to go with him upon the Mount of Olives, where he would show them how, upon his command, the walls of Jerusalem would fall down. Felix marched his soldiers out, and ordered them to attack the people; four hundred were cut down, but the Egyptian escaped. (*Ibid.* 8, § 6.) Thus, then, there was sufficient pretext for the Romans, as fully shown both by the character of Pilate and the tendency of the Roman rule in general, to condemn and execute Jesus for political reasons.

On the other hand, we are met, in this respect, by two great, irreconcilable contradictions in the accounts of the Evangelists. They relate, very fully, that Pilate had found Jesus not guilty, and exerted himself, with all his power, to save him, but that the Jewish people had persistently demanded, with wild clamor, the death of Jesus, and that Pilate had yielded *from fear of the peo- ple.* Then the narrative of the indignities offered to Jesus, and of his execution, follows. According to Matthew (xxvii.) Pilate resorted to this means to save Jesus: Being wont to release, on that feast, to the people any prisoner they chose, he offered them the choice between a notable robber and rebel, named Barabbas, and Jesus. But the people asked for Barabbas, and demanded the crucifixion of Jesus. Pilate alleged that he was innocent, but the people still persisted upon their demand. Pilate had water brought to him, washed his hands before the multitude, saying, "I am innocent of the blood of this just man ; see ye to it." Then answered *all* the people, and said, "His blood be on us, and on our children." Indeed, Matthew adduces still another motive prompting Pilate to save Jesus. He relates that, while he was sitting on the judgment seat, his wife sent to him, saying, " Have thou nothing to do with that just man; for I have suf- fered many things this day in a dream, because of him." Mark relates the same occurrence, except the dream of Pilate's wife, and his washing his hands, but, on the other hand, he elaborates the negotiations between the governor and the multitude. Luke (xxiii.) narrates that Pilate, after having declared to the people that he found no fault in Jesus, and having heard that he was a Gallilean, sent him to Herod, to whom Gallilee belonged, and that the latter, seeing Jesus would not answer his questions, sent him back again to Pilate. Then the governor once more alleged Jesus' innocence before the multitude, adding that he would chas- tize and then release him; but the people would not yield. Pi- late then did the same thing for the third time ; but the people persisted in their demand. Then Pilate resolved to yield to their clamor. According to John (xviii.) Pilate, at the beginning, said to the people, "Take him, and judge him according to your law;" whereupon the Jews replied, " It is not lawful for us to put any man to death." (Was it for the Jews to tell the governor this fact?) The Evangelists repeat several times that Pilate *feared* the people, and for that reason ordered the execution of Jesus ; nay, that he had him scourged and presented to them thus disfig- ured, with the view to excite their compassion ; but all in vain.

Let us now examine these two evident contradictions. The first refers to the hatred and blood-thirstiness of the Jewish people. The same people that, a day before, received Jesus with a festive procession, and paid him the most exquisite homage; of whom the priests, the Sanhedrin, and Pharisees were *afraid*, so that they would not lay hands on Jesus; that gave him the power to act the part of a master in the Temple of God, and drive from its courts the whole crowd of traders and venders, together with all their followers: the same people stand, on the day following, before the judgment-seat of the governor, clamor most terribly for the blood of Jesus, refuse all requests, repudiate all compassion, prefer the release of a " notable robber," and even invoke the curse upon their own heads and the heads of their children. And here it must be remembered that the people prepared that triumph for the popular speaker and the Messiah, and must, therefore, have known what they were doing. However changeable the temperament of a populace may be in general, we have here a contradiction which proves the statement of a fact to be untrue.—Still greater is the second contradiction, that Pilate, who, as we have seen, was merciless and relentless, even in matters of little account, who hated and despised the Jewish people, and most cruelly treated them on every occasion, who punished and suppressed, with the severest atrocity, every popular commotion and riot, all at once appears as the weakest coward, and delivers a man whom he publicly declares to be innocent, and makes all exertions to save, to his soldiers, for the most atrocious indignities, and the most agonizing execution, simply because the congregated rabble wildly clamored for his death. Nay, if Pilate had indeed been such a contemptible coward, how could he have *thus* compromised the dignity of his office, the authority of the Roman rule? If he would, indeed, yield to the populace from fear, must he not, at least, have saved the appearance, so that he did not make the weakness of his own power, and that of the Romans, still more manifest, by his repeated attempts to change the determination of the multitude, and his frequent protestations of the innocence of Jesus? He thus appears not only as the most miserable coward, who, from fear, makes himself the executioner of an innocent man, but also as the most contemptible representative of the Roman power. Indeed, Pilate ought to have met the Jewish people with vigorous resistance, to avoid the charge of weakness, and would, undoubtedly, in this respect, have been justified by the Roman authorities, if he had been accused of having spared the life of a rebel against the Roman government. But what was, in truth, done? Was he not, shortly after the execution of Jesus, accused of precisely the reverse, of relentless severity against the Jews, and, for that reason, sent by Vitellius to Rome to defend himself, whereas the latter acted with the most affable indulgence and consideration for the Jews? (*Josephus Antiq.* xviii. 4, § 3.)

Indeed,—we find here that which generally happens,—men go too far in their zeal to strengthen the belief in a cause, and thus refute it themselves. It is evident that it was intended to clear the Romans from the guilt of the death of Jesus, and charge it altogether upon the Jews. Therefore it is represented that Romans performed his execution reluctantly, and from fear of the Jewish people. For, considering that the powerless party of the Sanhedrin and Pharisees could not have awakened that fear, the Jewish people, the raging populace, had to be brought to act in the drama; the more the attempts of the Romans to save Jesus were prolonged, the more innocent did *they* appear, and the more guilty the Jews. Dreams, washing of hands, imprecations were called into requisition, with the view to emphasize the innocence of the Romans and the guilt of the Jews. But the narrators did not see that, while they made themselves more credible in the eyes of those who *would* find the Jews guilty, they entangled themselves in contradictions, which rendered the fiction evident and their motives manifest to all who will and can see clearly. It was necessary to represent the Jews as a terrible power, before which their own leaders and judges trembled on one day, and the Roman governor and his legions on the next following. The same Jews had to be represented on one day as filled with glowing enthusiasm for, and on the very next with blood-thirsty rage against, Jesus; and, lastly, a Roman captain, who is known to have possessed a relentless, obstinate character, who had ten times before mercilessly cut down the Jewish masses, had to be degraded to the level of a murderous tool, without a will of his own. Who, then, will hesitate to erase this whole scene from *history?*

The more clearly the motives of the scene described stand out in bold relief, the more it becomes manifest that still another act had to precede that scene. The people could not have been represented as having come to its raving madness of itself; it must needs have been brought, by the proceedings of its superiors and leaders, to a trial and condemnation of Jesus; but very little historical credibility attaches to the accounts of these proceedings. Our proofs for this assertion are as follows: 1. First of all, such a trial, with a sentence of death resulting therefrom on account of *religious opinions*, is without parallel in the history of the Jews, and it cannot be shown that the Jewish Sanhedrin thus made themselves judges of faith. The divers religious views of the then existing parties, of the Pharisees, Sadducees, and Essenes, and their manifold branches, the oftentimes diametrically opposed interpretations of the Academies of Shammai and Hillel had produced such a spirit of toleration, in matters of creed, that it only ended at a point where flagrant violations of the law and political tendencies commenced. There are instances recorded in history, showing that judicial condemnations, on account of violations of the law, did take place, and they were not at all times in strict accordance with the provisions of the penal law, but went beyond them under the influence of party passion; but none are recorded on account of religious opinion. Especially, as far as the Messianic idea is concerned, it never assumed such a character, however powerfully the popular heart was moved by it, that it caused judicial prosecutions, and the men who presented themselves as Messiahs were never persecuted by the Jewish authorities, but always by the Roman governors, as the examples above cited show. Nay, even the history of the Apostles furnish a proof for our statement, as it relates that, when Peter and John were made prisoners, and brought before the Sanhedrin, on account of their addresses to the people, the court released them upon the protest of Gamaliel, that religious opinions must not be made the subject of judicial cognizance and decision, but be left to the judgment of God. (*Acts* v. 34, &c.)*

2. The Gospel according to John knows nothing at all of the

---

* The same is confirmed also in the account of the death of Jacobus in *Josephus Antiq.* xx. 9, § 1.

judicial proceedings, of the examination of witnesses, of the interrogatories put to the accused and his condemnation, of all of which the other Evangelists present such a full account. After having related (xi. 47) that the high-priests and Pharisees had first counselled together to put Jesus to death, it gives an account of the arrest of Jesus, (chapter xviii.,) tells us that Jesus was at first led to Annas, the former high-priest, who asked him " of his disciples and of his doctrines," whereupon Jesus pointed to the fact that he had openly taught in the Synagogue and in the Temple. Hereupon Jesus was brought before Caiaphas, who sent him before Pilate. With the exception of the account of Peter's denial of Christ, this is all that John narrates until his appearance before Pilate ; hence there is not the least trace to be found in his Gospel of a judicial proceeding before the Sanhedrin. If the accounts of the other three Evangelists did not exist, we could derive no other conclusion from John than this, that a number of Pharisees, in connection with the high-priest, had secretly conspired against Jesus, and then delivered him up to the Roman governor. His silence on such an important act, which is of the greatest weight in the examination of the life of Jesus, and his condemnation, cannot but essentially strengthen our doubts of the historical truth of the real occurrence of the facts related. This silence of John justifies our assumption that the accounts of the other Evangelists are but embellishments, without any historic value whatever.

3. The accounts contain a number of contradictions in themselves with each other, and with the Jewish law. Even the arrest of Jesus presents some doubts. The band commissioned with its execution is said to have consisted of servants of the high-priest and the Sanhedrin, and, nevertheless, to have found it necessary to employ a traitor, not alone to designate the place where Jesus had spent the night, but also to point him out among his disciples. According to the three Evangelists, Judas kissed Jesus to give them a sign: "Whomsoever I shall kiss that same is he ; hold him fast." According to John, Jesus went to meet them, and asked them: "Whom seek ye?" And when they answered him by calling out his name, he continued: "I am he ;" whereupon they repeatedly "fell to the ground." Can it be imagined
5

that the servants and messengers of the priests and Sanhedrin should not have known the man whose preaching in the Temple and whose appearance before the eyes of the people had created such great commotion? Is it possible that there was not even one amongst all the servants of the highest court of the Jews who should have known him, so that a paid traitor and such special proceedings were required to effect his arrest? These questions become the more emphatic and important when we consider that but a little while after two maid-servants of the house of the high-priest recognised Peter as one of Jesus' disciples, and designated him as such, in spite of his repeated denial. If the disciple of Jesus was thus generally known as such, how can it be possible that his master was not equally generally known? This contradiction vanishes when we recognise the band who arrested him, not as servants of the Jewish authorities, but as Roman soldies, who, indeed, required a Jewish guide, as whom the traitor Judas presented himself. And John actually designated them as Romans, saying (xviii. 3): "Judas then received the band of men and officers from the chief priests and Pharisees," and verse 12: "Then the band and the captain and officers of the Jews took Jesus." Thus, then, the captain and the real band were Roman soldiers, who were accompanied by several Jewish officials, so that the arrest of Jesus was an act of the Roman governor, and not of the Jewish court. The mention of *high-priests*—in the plural number—(*e. g.* Matthew xxxi. 3, 14) is in conflict with the Jewish institutions. Matthew xxvii. 1 speaks even of "*all*" the high-priests. John repeatedly speaks even of the high-priest of "that same year;" for instance, in chapter xxviii. verse 13, he says: Καιαφας ὁς ἦν ἀρχιερευς του ἐνιαυτου ἐκεινου, "who was the high-priest that same year?" as though there was an annual rotation in the office of the high-priest, whereas Caiaphas held that office without interruption during the whole administration of Pilate, that is to say, ten years. This shows a great ignorance of the Jewish institutions which, it is easy to explain, existed a century after the discontinuance of that office. But who was this Caiaphas? The Rabbins know no high-priest of that name at all; only two centuries later a similar name—Joseph of Chaipha—is mentioned. Nor do Mark and Luke know that name, but speak only of a high-priest; only Matthew (xxvi. 3) says: "The high-priest, who was called Caiaphas;" and mentions his name also in chapter xxvii. 57. This name is found also in John xi. 49, xxviii. 13, 24. Now, Josephus mentions one Joseph upon whom the governor, Gratus, conferred the office of high-priest, and of whom it was taken again by Vitellius, after the fall of Pilate. Hence the execution of Jesus could have taken place only under the pontificate of this Joseph. In both passages of Josephus the name of Joseph is followed by "ὁ και Καιαφας," (Antiq. xviii. 2, § 2,) and (4, § 3) "τον και Καιαφαν ἐπικαλούμενον," "who was also called Caiaphas," an addition which we regard as an interpolation made with the view to place the high-priest Caiaphas mentioned by the two Evangelists on a historical basis.

But the greatest objections grow out of the dates given, the variety of which creates various doubts when compared with the law of the Jews. All four Evangelists agree in this, that the resurrection of Jesus took place on a Sunday, and that his body rested in the grave on the Sabbath preceding. But how do the Evangelists represent all the rest? In the first consultation, the Sanhedrin are said to have agreed not to proceed against Jesus "on a feast-day, lest there be an uproar among the people." (Matthew xxvi. 5, Mark xiv. 2.) Did they thus seek to avoid all commotion of the people? Or did they fear the people might rebel against them, for a violation by them of a solemn feast? And should they have, nevertheless, proceeded against Jesus on the feast-day, and thus stirred up a commotion of the people? Matthew relates that the Passover meal was prepared for Jesus "on the first day of the feast of unleavened bread" (Matthew xxvi. 17); that he celebrated it "when the even was come;" that in the night he was arrested, tried, and sentenced; that in the morning he was carried before Pilate and executed, and in the evening laid into the grave. Thus, then, a two-fold inconsistency is presented: that the day preceding the feast is called "the first of the feast of unleavened bread," and that his trial and execution took place on the first day of Passover.

But this is in conflict with the Jewish law, as we have already seen, and would be a direct violation of the solemn feast, for which hundreds of thousands of Jewish men poured into Jerusa-

lem, and which was celebrated with extraordinary distinction.—
But verse 62 of chapter xxvii. causes a difficulty, saying: "Now,
the next day that followed the day of preparation," the Pharisees
sealed the sepulchre that it was made sure. What does "the day
after the day of preparation" mean? Only the day of preparation for the Sabbath (eve of Sabbath) can have been meant; for
the day of preparation for Passover was long past, and "the
next day that followed the day of preparation" would be the
Sabbath itself, which could hardly be thus designated, and on
which the Pharisees were not permitted to seal the sepulchre.—
Thus, then, there was a confusion of ideas that renders all very
enigmatical. Mark agrees with Matthew, but says (xv. 42) that
after Jesus had expired, "Now, when the even was come, (because it was the preparation, that is, the day before the Sabbath,) Joseph of Arimathea got permission to bury the body of
Jesus." According to this statement, Friday would have been
the day of the execution, and, at the same time, the day of Passover. Luke relates more correctly: "Then came the day of unleavened bread, when the Passover must be killed." (xxii. 7).
This, then, was the preparation of Passover. After the break
of day—thus he relates—the trial took place, and on the same
day also the execution. This, then, was the day of Passover.
The same day, he tells us, in chapter xxiii. 54, was the preparation of Sabbath—hence Friday. Farther, he relates also, that
on the same day women prepared spices and ointments for the
corpse, to use them on Sunday, and that they "rested on the
Sabbath-day according to the commandment" (v. 56). The incon-
sistencies of all these proceedings on the feast of Passover are
thus increased by another, to wit: that the women prepared ointments on the feast-day, in violation of the law, whereas they observed the Sabbath conscientiously. John does not at all agree
with the three other Evangelists. He relates that Jesus took
supper with his disciples in the evening of the 13th of Nissan.
This, then, was either the Passover supper, taken at a time not
commanded by the Jewish law, or it was only an ordinary supper,
which Jesus distinguished by washing the feet of his disciples.—
According to John, the arrest and execution of Jesus took place
on the 14th day of Nissan, hence on the day preceding the feast,

which was, at the same time, Friday, that is, the preparation of Sabbath (xiii. 29, xxiii. 28, xix. 31); so that the first day of Passover occurred on the Sabbath. This arrangement contains nothing in conflict with the Jewish law, but the supper thus loses the character of a Passover meal upon which the other three Evangelists tenaciously insist; and hence another contradiction is presented: the latter gives a full narrative of the preparation of the Passover supper at the house of a man in the city, whereas, according to the account of John, it did not take place at all.

Thus, then, the result of our investigation is simply this: The trial and condemnation of Jesus by the Sanhedrin, and the demand of his death by the Jewish people, lack every historical authority. On the contrary, Jesus was arrested and executed, as many other Messiahs who at that time presented themselves as such before the Jews, by the Roman procurator, because the commotion stirred up among the people by these pretenders appeared politically dangerous in the eyes of the Romans.*  That

---

* The result arrived at by the author is still more strengthened, if not placed beyond all doubt and contradiction, when we consult the ancient Roman law in connection with the trial, condemnation, and execution of Jesus; for we shall then find that the view taken by Pilate of his offence, the punishment inflicted, and the forms observed at his execution, *in all their details,* were altogether in accordance with the ancient law of Rome.

The greatest punishment was crucifixion. (*Pauli,* sent. rec. lib. v. tit. 17 § 3: *Summa supplicia sunt cruce,* &c.) The highest and most heinous crime was that of *perduellio,* which comprised all offences against the peace and security of the commonwealth, such as treason, rebellion, conspiracy, usurpation of political power and authority, &c. Even at a later period, when the term *crimen majestatis* was used in law for all political offences, the crime of *perduellio* was still retained as distinct from the whole class. (l. 11 D. xlviii. 4.) To perfect the crime it was not a necessary condition than an overt act should have been committed; mere treasonable language, disclosing the intention of the person, was sufficient to render him guilty of the crime. (*Pauli,* sent. l. c. tit. 19 § 1; l. 4 pr. l. 10 D. l. 7 § 3; D. 48, 4; l. 11 cit: *Hostili animo adversus rem publicam vel principem animatus.*) Whoever was found guilty of *perduellio* was bound, scourged, and hanged with his head covered. (C. F. Dieck, *Historical Essays on the Criminal Law of the Romans:* Halle, 1822, page 4-44.) Here we may at once add, that the death-penalty for the *crimen majestatis* was at one time abolished, but restored again and executed, with all its appendages, under the emperors, against the Christian martyrs found guilty of holding secret conventions, of believing in those who had been crucified for political crimes, such as sedition, *usurpation of royalty,* &c. (Rudorff, *History of*

the information given to Pilate originated with the Jews, and
that a Jew, and even a disciple of Jesus, lent himself for the
especial purpose to point him out, we will admit; and these very
facts may be regarded as the real sum and substance of the whole
picture of the scenes before the Sanhedrin and the judgment
seat of Pilate. *But an actual trial before the Sanhedrin never
took place, nor was there ever a clamorous demand by the Jewish
people for the execution of Jesus*, so that the Jews cannot be regarded as the authors of the death of Jesus and be charged with
it. As long as the commotion stirred up by Jews was confined

*the Roman Law*, vol. ii., page 369.) It was this very crime of usurpation of
royalty, of preaching rebellion, in a word, of *perduellio*, of which Jesus was
tried before Pilate, of which he was convicted (Matthew xxvii. 11, Mark xv.
2, &c., &c.), and for which he was crucified according to the Roman law.—
Before he was executed he was bound (it is true, the Gospels tell us that the
Jews bound him, which, however, appears to be incorrectly recorded) and
scourged, and then crucified. (Matthew xxvii. 26, Mark xv. 15, &c.) While
in Rome certain officers—the *duumviri, quæstores*, &c.—superintended executions, this task was committed in the provinces to a *centurio;* the execution
itself was performed by a *speculator, (Seneca*, de ira. i. 16, *Dion*. lxxviii. 14,
l. 6 D. 48, 20,) or by assistants—*optiones*—such as soldiers, &c., chosen by the
*centurio* (l. 6 cit.; Varro, L. L. v. 16). We find the *centurio* and his soldier
assistants at the execution of Jesus. (Matthew xxvii. 27, 54, Mark xv. 16, 39,
&c., &c. The speculator—σπεκουλατωρ—is mentioned in Mark vi. 27). In
Rome there were certain places designated for executions; in the provinces
they were performed in the suburbs. (*Dion* viii. 78, l. 25 § 1, D. 48, 10; *Livius*
viii. 15, *Suet*. Tib. 61.) Jesus was executed on Golgotha. (Matthew xxvii. 33,
Mark xv. 22.)

The garments with which a culprit was clothed when he was carried to his
execution—*spolia*—could be kept by the executioner, whereas all other effects
that he had with him—*pannicularia*—were either delivered to the *fiscus* or
employed by the *præses* for other purposes, (l. 6 D. xlviii. 20.) We see from
the Gospels that the soldiers stripped Jesus and put on him a scarlet robe, and
after his death parted his garments, (Matthew xxvii. 28, 35, &c., &c.,) which
latter act, however, is interpreted in a way to suit a certain reference to a
verse in Psalm xxii.,—the tendency of this reference may be seen from the
fact that king David is called a prophet.

Lastly, that the body of Jesus was delivered to Joseph of Arimathea, (Matthew xxvii. 57, Mark xv. 43, &c., &c.,) was also in accordance with the Roman law, which provided that the body of an executed criminal should be
delivered to his relatives, or to any person that demanded it. (Dig. 48, 24:
*De cadaveribus punitorum.*)

We cannot here elaborate upon this subject. The above sketch will be sufficient for the purpose indicated at the beginning of this note.—TRANSLATOR.

within the province of Gallilee, no notice was taken of it; but when he dared to present himself even in Jerusalem as the Messiah, and thus created a commotion among the people, which, happening under his own eyes, could not remain secret from the ever suspectful Pilate, the latter had the author of that commotion arrested, while his own disciples betrayed him. With this act the political side of the events turned up, and the Jews were the more compelled to disavow all connection with Jesus, as they had to fear the worst from Pilate. But Pilate sought indeed to implicate the Jews in the movements of Jesus, as shown by his speeches and the inscription over the cross drafted by him, because he thereby hoped to gain a new weapon against them to be used in his defence against the accusations of cruelty pending against him before the court of Rome. But even because the doctrine of Jesus was more of an ethic nature, and partly beyond the comprehension of the people, the latter soon deserted him, and Pilate could find no one besides Jesus to apprehend and punish. And this circumstance explained also the silence of Josephus. The event did not affect the people at large: only one individual suffered thereby.

Having found that the motive for implicating the Sanhedrin and the Jewish people to be this, to charge the guilt of the death of Jesus upon the Jews, and to exculpate the Romans as much as possible: it is not difficult to perceive also the object at the bottom thereof. It is a notorious fact, that Christianity found no favor at all among the Jewish people; the number of Jesus' disciples had but little increased, and wherever the Apostles presented themselves before the Jewish people they were rejected. Hence the hope to convert the Jews, or even a considerable portion of them, had to be dismissed, and the proper scene of conversion had to be removed into the midst of the heathen nations. But then it was of vital importance to controvert the belief that Jesus had been executed by Roman authorities as a political criminal and public enemy, to present it, on the contrary, as a false insinuation by the Jews, and to show that the Roman judge was fully convinced of the innocence of the accused, but was forced to yield to the obstinate clamors of the Jews. It was naturally a matter of indifference in what light Pilate himself would appear in the construction of the events, as long as it was stated that he was all along convinced of the innocence of Jesus, and publicly manifested his conviction by the ceremony of washing his hands. Thereby another object was accomplished: Judaism was thus represented as completely different from Christianity, and the votaries of the former as separated from those of the latter before the eyes of the heathens, a distinction which had become more and more important for the representatives of Christianity. The representation that the condemnation of Jesus emanated from the Sanhedrin naturally proved clearly, that it could have originated only in a full difference, nay, in an antagonism between the two doctrines; for the death of Jesus thus appeared not to have been caused by the caprice of a rebellious people, but by the decision of the great body of the teachers of the law.— And here also it was a matter of indifference, that the breach between Judaism and Christianity was widened by this representation. This breach had been caused by the very death of Jesus, because it confuted the messianic dignity of Jesus, according to the ideas which the Jews of that time entertained of the Messiah.

———

The labors of modern historical criticism number but few decades. But they have kindled their torch, and not only illumine with it many hitherto dark portions of the history of mankind, but carry their light also into such that have hitherto ·appeared lucid and clear. And thus it becomes manifest that many forms, events, and epochs had been seen in false reflection, that often light and shadow had been unjustly and incorrectly distributed. Such is the task of modern historical criticism,—it is often troublesome, even painful, often attended with violent and protracted struggles; but it is the grander and the more beatific, the more fearlessly and perseveringly it strives, step by step, to approach the truth, to destroy the errors of the past, and to create or restore true knowledge. It will be assaulted, condemned, anathematized; but if it will understand how to guard itself against excesses and exaggerations, or abandoning its results too soon, it will be recognised, appreciated, and admired. The principles of justice, the authority of which modern time strives more and more to establish, are employed also for retrospection, and will remove all ignominy and prejudice from those upon whom they had been unjustly heaped. The spirit of true liberty penetrates also into the crypts and charnel-houses of the past, and cleans them from the foul vapors that were collected there, because they were kept closed and walled up. Let us not become discouraged because progress is but slow, and all labor appears at times to be in vain. All that exists through the process of history is of great weight and persistent tenacity, and can be purified and revived only through history itself. Our fathers labored for us, and we labor for our posterity.